SEVENTY-FIVE
THINGS **BLACK** PEOPLE
WON'T STOP DOING...

Gun Crime

Stealing

Cheating

The amount of time that goes bye in doing such things!
When we could be learning how to . . .
Love Each Other

SEVENTY-FIVE
THINGS **BLACK** PEOPLE
WON'T STOP DOING...

Greetings, in the name of the most High God King an Creator, His Imperial Majesty Emporia Haile Sellassie I King of all Kings Lord of all Lords Conquering Lion of the Tribe of Judah, the most high King

Jah Rastafari

RANDY SIMONS

iUniverse, Inc.
Bloomington

Seventy-Five Things Black People Won't Stop Doing . . .

iUniverse books may be ordered through booksellers or by contacting:

iUniverse
1663 Liberty Drive
Bloomington, IN 47403
www.iuniverse.com
1-800-Authors (1-800-288-4677)

ISBN: 978-1-4759-5546-0 (sc)
ISBN: 978-1-4759-5410-4 (hc)
ISBN: 978-1-4759-5545-3 (ebk)

Library of Congress Control Number: 2012918907

Printed in the United States of America

iUniverse rev. date: 10/04/2012

ACKNOWLEDGMENT

This book has not been put together to offend or belittle any one in any way, so to whom so ever it may strike a chord with my warmest regards, apologies to you. We humans don't like to be told we are doing something wrong, most of all not by someone who looks just like you, that in it self can be a real danger for all involved.

Untold amounts of troubles and pain, individually and for society as a whole most of all for a certain people in society, say one race in the making mention of such facts let's hope a real change can come about, if anything let it viewed in the humor it is intended to portray and hour alone, these findings having been put together with in and throughout three different countries, USA, LONDON and BERMUDA even parts of the carbine.

There is no one involved in the making of this book who feels or has a thought that he or she is better than anyone else on this our planet Earth, no matter where you is from. So, to whom so ever these words may strike a chord with, you have my regards, you me sorry. This life we a live no one can denied,

In spite of the ease to not become all that we can be let us make and effort to live in love.

Even though living by a set format can seem regimental, somewhat tiring, the end result can't be denied. Neither can one denied the benefits thereof. Everything within this our Universe exists in a constant due to it abiding by a set format. As chaotic and violent as it is, it's a set format. The end result of that format gives us life on this planet Earth.

So, think may be some real mystic occurrences should be able to occur through human interaction, of mutual consent, there by making our interaction a heartfelt, real action.

Remember Iron sharpens Iron, so does the intellect of one man will sharpen the other, how much more magic must be able to occur, if we base our association on heart felt basis.

MORALS AND PRINCIPLES

These two can and will set standards whether high or low depends on the level of enforcement one stands by in implementing these two.

In the implementing of such things in one's daily life can only make life brighter in many ways for the individual and those with in one's circle. It can also have a real effect on society as a whole. In denying such things if you will agree is to live like you is less than human, due to the mannerism that can develop sight.

In many black house holds in the fifties an sixties the enforcement of these things was a constant. In some cases the enforcement of such things was community effort up held by all adults in the community. Some parts of the world even if you went out of your community an tried to denied having any knowledge of morals and principles, you would soon find that lots of people stood by such things.

Making your actions more noticeable by many. It has been said many times by many people that, life repeats itself, so let us take aim at our former glory an remember; you get outa life what you put in it, along the way let it be pointed out, that there is strength in numbers if I show you love and in turn you show love to the next black person, we can't miss.

It's a fact, that ain't no one love you, like you love yourself, an loving your sister an brother can fit such a chant, cause them black just like you. We've made many changes through this life were living, from Kings and Queens to slaves and then back to some of the richest people in society and still we never really along the way clung to each other as a people, As Black People.

Such an effort can be made right in the family home so as to watch the benefit of the enforcement of standards and principles, the turnaround effect it will have on the individual the effect it will have on the BLACK RACE as a nation as a people.

The black neighborhoods, black cities, black countries think about it. This not being a thing that can only be incomprehensible but a thing of attain ability cause we done did it already. Time and time aging from as far back as I can remember an that's over forty years Black people the world over have repeatedly ignored certain standards an the virtues to be had by the constant enforcement of these standards within the family home.

Just the other day in the eighteen hundreds a vast majority of us could not read or write and many of us had no type of wealth at all. You could say most of the black race was poor by society's standards; to go back even further would give an even clearer pic of where we should strive to go as a race of people.

Let's start with Timbuktu, of which was built by us, order an manner even the standard of life in these city walls was put in place by us black people. We lived in peace an love fe true, our cities where places of habitation an livety we abode by guidelines an order every aspect of life in side of these city dwellings was put in place by us black people.

As to maintain life an a continual existence on this planet earth. A very high standard of integrity was proclaimed in having black skin.

It was not until some of the many visitors to our shores got bright and took advantage of our relaxed manner toward new faces. Of which was used against us to the extent of the collapse of our many cities throughout time. This having occurred so often we started to live in smaller cities and then in huts and villages, right in to the trees, hence the pic a vast majority of black people have of African descent. A manner stuck to so as to get through. for as soon as we built up our cities, them all a come mash it down!

So in our small communities an little hut villages we stayed alive. As if that wasn't enough they came and started to steal us away from Africa. Taken us to every part of the world, where in they wanted to live, put chains around our necks hands and ankles, [but that's another story] so having walked through life from then till now we stand here in the Twenty second century our Owen worst enemy.

In the manner we do things to one another an our self's we do things as if we must fight our brother; the next black man has to be our enemy. We, kill we one another, steal from each other, all manner of things to one another, all too often it seems we can only do such things to other black people. Not saying other races don't get in on the mayhem of denying us.

Saying if we stop fighting one another that'll be half the fight won. The many things we can attain to if we stop fighting one another, I mean look around you, there aren't no more enemy out there to stop our progress. All other races have finally stopped enslaving us, exploiting us and fighting us.

To keep us off the stage of productivity and progress, shoot all other races want to be just like us in every aspect them want dress like we, the hanging pants, over size clothes shoes, even dread locks dem want to wear.

So having said all that it can be said the oldest civilization on this planet, Social living even brotherly love an social inclusion, love and progress started with in our home land mother Africa many years ago.

Within Africa in these many ruins utensils for eating have been found tools for cooking food have been found even evidence to show food was harvested and stored in abundance.

We black people have always lived a progressive an productive life as a people as a race we loved we one another even in the face of our minor differences. Having walked through life an reaching where we stand today as a race of people we still outnumber any other race we are still counted as the strongest race on this planet earth.

We still lead all other races in mostly every aspect of social living, fashion, talk, humor even religion.

In showing you I intend not to offend or belittle any one in any way but I'm pointing out these facts that we can smile at these things in humor then we can look to change them.

Yo, no matter where you come from as long as your skin is black you are faced with the same set of obstacles as the black man living in the streets. Just remove a few layers of your protective covering an woo be unto you, financially secure Mr. black man and woman.

So having said all that lets take a look at religion. Most religions derive from the same stock, a big number of them have real similar stories in their holy books. Throughout them all, there is one where in god presents Himself as a man amongst men with a family tree of which can be traced right back to the start of this religious awareness.

Coming right up to date solidifying the fact that man was made in the Image of God. In his likeness the Most High King and Creator Jah Rastafari.

0) THEY WON'T PULL TOGETHER AS A PEOPLE,

thus no matter where you come from if your skin is black, brown even yella you are considered a black person.

We have no community adhesiveness an nor do we take time to acknowledge that the road blocks that were used to stop a certain amount of black people from getting xyz today will be used in so many months to come stop a brand new batch.

Where in pulling together as a people would prevent that on many levels.

Pulling together would solidified everything we are due on many levels where in what I get every black person coming behind me can't be denied.

1) VERY SELDOM, IN MOST CASES
THEY WON'T PULL TOGETHER AS A COMMUNITY

With in many cities throughout the world there are areas where in just black people live, but we still fight one another an do our out most to stop each other from progressing on many different levels many times in such cases there is very little or none at all private matters with in such settings due to our ease dropping medalling or outright inquiring, an once we have accomplished a search of such degree our findings becomes the neighborhood conversation over an over aging we are our Owen worst enemy.

Many ghettos of the world are filled with black people where in it should be easier for unity to be achieved.

It's as easy as ill look out for yours when you're not around an you look out for mine when im not around.

I'll love you like I love myself an I'll make a effort to acknowledge your presents in our day to day passing.

2) THEY WON'T PULL TOGETHER IN NO FORM OF INTERNATIONAL BUSINESS

For the many things we can pick up an deliver to the world having been funded by us alone.

We haven't done an are not trying to do.

Mind you there is more than enough money in black people's pockets to do such things if we where to come together.

So it seems that our biggest joy is in knowing that our neighbor is in the same or worst finical state as us.

There can be choice in such a venture in light of the many things that can be put in place. end

3) THEY WON'T PULL TOGETHER IN DEMAND FOR ANY FORM OF COMPENSATION FOR THE DEGRADATION OF SLAVERY

Every other race on this our planet earth that has been through any form of decoration or some form of forced labor from another race has taken their issues to some court an been awarded some amount of financial compensation for their suffering an torment along with any life that was lost along the way, yes other races have been payed some have got paid more than once.

Please note that whatever suffering or torment other races have went through have been minor compared to slavery.

Compensation for slavery should be awarded due to the long genetic effects it has dispersed.

Shoot we still bow to anything lighter than us, NOT TRUE?

4) THEY DON'T DEMAND MORE ACADEMIC PERFORMANCE FROM THEIR CHILDREN DURING THEIR PUBLIC SCHOOL YEARS

Most black people send their children to public schools an statics will show that our children time an time aging en up on the bottom of THE ladder academically.

Such things have taken place from our release from slavery up to date 2010.

Very little mot times none at all nurturing is given to our children's primary education many times this goes over in to secondary school all too often secondary school is walked away from by male an female black people.

Sadly this is allowed by black parents time an time aging.

From way back when to date.

Many have been told the same thing; you may as well leave [school] now, go get a job;.

5) THEY WON'T PULL TOGETHER IN ILLEGAL DEALINGS.

For the many communities throughout the world where in black people sell drugs not one can say that they see to each other's well being in any one of those communities.

See to each other in the manner as to see to it that families have food tidy clothes for the yard an school.

Even transport to get to school regularly all the same time trying to keep the illegal activity hidden from the youth of these communities.

In most cases the main customer are the people in the communities.

And that's drugs of all sorts.

Lots of times in many cities you'll find three even more Individuals of whom will never see any sort of money if They didn't buy an sell the neighborhood crave.

Drugs most in demand.

But they'll never put their money together to increase their in take or even work together to increase their ability to supply.

6) They won't capitalize on style an fashion of which the world walks in comes from black people.

From there ass hanging out to hot pants black people start dress like that first.

There are many forms of dress that where stared by lack people as a neighborhood dress of which was picked up by some other race mass produce an sold back to us.

This being the case on many different levels of dress in society. From official bunn to just hanging in the hood.

Take a look around. We've always wore clothes as a race of people to a high level of class.

7) They don't an won't help an pull one another through society. For the many educated an professional.

Black people, out there in society they won't an have never made it known to the poorer blacks, the many legal avenues they can take to change their situations financially from a legal stand point.

Within an throughout many cities of the world lots of black people don't have a clue about the many help agencies in their cities. Yet time an time aging, the few educated professionals ones who may know will not neither have they taken any steps to make it known to the general black population of the legal loop holes in society.

There are help agencies in most cities of the world to assist people to get from A to B this being life's standards.

You'll find many of these are rarely known of by the general public of black people even in cases where a person may just need access to a dry place to sleep an running water so as to maintain a upful appearance in society, many times black people will deny other black people.

8) THEY ACCEPT BEING DENIED PROGRESS

Some what of a feeble statement to make in light of the state of life as we know it to date.

Still who feels it knows it and them and those of whom who has had to absorb all the torment that comes with being denied will

Admit to the maneuvering that can take place in order to denied them theirs, not true?

9) THEY DON'T EXERCISE ANY FORM OF PROFESSIONALISM IN MANY ASPECTS OF BUSINESS. YOU CAN FINED IN MANY INSTANCES.

In many forms of business when black people, business owners are approached by another black person who is not known to them, right away they think negative of new faces, no matter the new faces ability or qualifications.

Right away the new face is put in a criteria an denied chance to grow financial an character in the content of daily association with people. [as is said in the bible iron sharpen nest iron] As with people one mans character will strengthen the next mans character in many different ways.

In such actions the new face is made to live under his or her standard due to not being able to earn his net worth.

10) DUE TO THEIR DESIRE TO DO NOTHING IN SOCIETY THEY TRY TO JUSTIFY THEIR NEGATIVE ATTITUDES.

They make excuse after excuse, not to put out one percent in things they do, to justify their lazy attitudes.

A job interview, a hustle, even some one taking them to meet the boss of a work site, is all situations where in black people who want to do nothing will either, turn up late or won't turn up at all. An still act as though its someone else fault for them not getting the job or the person doing the hire ring is biases to them so they don't or didn't get the job.

Many times black people will destroy their chances before they even get going in the manner they will present them self's to the hire ring person.

11) They all to often copy other races in style language even eating habits even though other races want to be just like us.

Every six say seven out of ten men a women take up an copy other races in style eating habits an mannerism.

Constantly black people will deny their self worth an follow other races in many ways. In this action they start to execute many forms of prejudice toward other black people they even start to build a deep resentment toward certain categories of the black race.

Even pin pointing them as the cause of certain ills in society. If there is one race that can act like another is the black race.

12) AS A RACE A PEOPLE THEY HAVE THE MOST TEENAGE PREGNANCIES

in any part of the world Teenage black girls are more likely to get pregnant than other races.

This being encouraged by a older black person many times.

It seems like a hidden rule that a black young lady has had to have at least three most times two children by the age of twenty three.

All to often being left to bring up these children with their parents.

Often these young ladies having been encouraged away from school by the individual whom has help to make the child now no one has the mean of providing for the child.

Y o, can you tell of anyone this has not happen to from way back when up to date, without lying?

13) THEY ARE THE MAJORITY IN PRISONS
EVEN WHEN THEY ARE OUT NUMBERED IN MANY CITIES

Numbers show all over the world that black people are most likely to outnumber all other races in most prisons throughout society.

Most countries throughout the world have large numbers of black people in their prison male an female even in cases were black people are no the majority in society.

In some cases other races having been faced with some crimes that make us the majority are giving fines or even lesser penalties for their doings.[not jail] No its not just us running in there. Prisons.

14) THEY MAKE THE MOST NOISE IN PUBLIC PLACES, THAT GOES FOR CHILD TEENAGE AN ADULT.

Most places that have black communities all to often have the highest recorded number of public disorders it also can be seen an said that black people make the most noise in [public places all over the world.)

From a private conversation to a bloody altercation black people always tip the scale in noise.

Any one taken a quick look at the black race would thing they can't hear to good due to the excessive noise used to communicate between them on many different levels in many different situations.

15) In many communities through Out the world many Black youth In their eagerness to exert a domineering mannerism,

Tend to become THE majority in many prisons around the world, time an time aging in encountering such individuals You would think such people come from the same Walks of life, when actually these persons can be found On total opposites paths in this life, one pampered the Other from the ghettos this persona can be found in some black females also, Who end up going down the same type paths.

From Prison to the street, From the street back to prison. So (can't read) go, in more than (can't read).
All over the world

16) THEY RESORT TO BEING THE MOST UNPRODUCTIVE PEOPLE IN MANY ASPECTS OF SOCIETY LIFE.

Time an time aging they could be given opportunity to succeed in many different things an would fail many times they quit.

Many black people having someone to spend the day with doing nothing, they will look to be with that group regularly all to often they develop a frame of mind where is even their necessity has to be spoon fed to them.

Having said such it can be agreed that if such things are not put in place for them all manner of hostilities are released from the receiving persons.

All to often to real violent an argumentative extant.

17) They don't demand or protest for any type of recognition for the many

Contributes they have made to society as we know it to date. Many of so many thing's that are common place in today's world was designed by black people.

The whole concept of society living was designed by black people their origin comes out of Africa.

Many a great many different legislation were put in place to safe guard the continual existence of the whole race back in African cities.

They've given us one month.

18) THEY THINK A CONVERSATION IS TELLING SOMEONE ABOUT THEIR PRIVATE AFFAIRS.

In many cases they talk all their house hold affairs in public just to make conversation with people they know.

In turn this is done even when the house is not theirs an they don't have any form of occupancy in said house.

Detailed happenings an affairs are spoken in the street without discretions all to often.

If there is no change in house hold affairs then there is no conversation in the street.

Meaning if the house is constantly chaotic then them alright. SIGHT?

19) THEY DON'T TEACH THEIR CHILDREN THE IMPORTANCE OF MONEY MANAGEMENT.

In many cases all they do is put money in their children's hands fe go spend.

That being the case with the poor an professional black families.

Money management is all to often never taught in the black home.

This being a thing done generation after generation from back as far as you want go.

Nor is there any type of financial stepping stones put in place by child bearing Black people for those children they be having.

Many times a financial plan is never put in place by black people for the many children they bear.

Lots of times the money that is put in the children's hand is done so to a level as to insinuate the standard of life in these homes an as if to tell society there is lots of money in this house, hmm more than is in your house.

20) THEY WILL NOT LEAVE PHARMACEUTICAL DRUGS ALONE EVEN AFTER BEING SHOWN THE ILL EFFECTS THEY HAVE ON THE BODY.

In spite of the much available info in regards to herbal remedies' being provide by black doctors for black people they still run for the pharmaceutical drugs, still dem want take a pill to so dem say cure their ill.

Many of the pharmaceutical drugs given to black people really ingest totally in to the black humans system. In many cases pharmaceutical drugs from not totally ingesting in the body end up sitting elsewhere in the body.

If not ingested then it can't be passed out of the body.

21) Many times black people will turn to other races to materialize a vast amount of

Money making ventures before they will try with a black person.

Within an throughout the business world many blacks turn to people outside of the black race to materialize their money making ventures.

Many black people consider it high risk to go in to business with another black person.

Even if trailer loads of money is in one black man's hands other blacks will still join up with other races as if there some sort of guarantee they will progress in such ventures with other races.

22) ELDERLY BLACK PEOPLE ARE THE MOST PREJUDICE PEOPLE TO WARD YOUNG BLACK PEOPLE

Through out many cities of the world.

Elderly black people in many parts of the world act in a manner as if young black people can do no right. They won't give young black people a chance to prove them self's in many cases neither do they give a helping hand to young black people in situations of Financial ventures many a times.

Many black older people will proclaim a new young black face a thug before even given a chance for them to show their net worth.

In some black communities no form of communicate exist between elderly Black people an the youth. This can happen in some black families.

23) THEY HATE TO REPAY LOANS AN CLEAR UP DEBTS

Black people have the most debt in many different aspects of society even money owed to we one another.

In many cases they'll have the money an avoid the encounter of having to hand I over to clear up the dept.

Sometimes upon encounter violent occurrence take place aging to avoid clearing up the dept.

Attitude an response toward one another can change drastically when it comes to money amongst black people. Sometimes all to often lots of black friend ships will end over money being owed to someone.

Some black people will think they have succeed in some sort of trick, in having you put money in their hand as a loan. True them have no intent of paying you back.

24) They stay home with parents even after being of age to have their Owen place

Time an time aging you have black people well over twenty one in their parents' house with their children who in a lot of cases these children being over eighteen years of age.

Very little sometimes no effort is made to vacate the parents home.

Many times the day to day running of these houses are still maintained by the parent, the whole financial responsibility is carried by the parents.

In many cases the mother alone bears this load, so she lives penniless.

In lots of cases the mother choices are deemed trivial by all other occupants of her home, yet she is financial responsible for keeping this house paid for.

in lots of cities you can find mums making their way home at the end of the day with three or more bags of groceries, while the youngest occupant of many of these houses is sitting off playing with their children, mums grandchildren.

25) IF IN ANY COUNTRY A BLACK MAN TRIES TO STAND AGAINST INJUSTICE

The first to tell him not to or discouraged him form doing so is another Black man.

Many a times in many countries when a black person tries to fight the system he is persuade by other black people to "not do it."

A black man tries to make a stand against any form of in justice he is quickly faced with disassociation by many black people.

Even if his actions are to help the majority, even if he or she has not the ability to discern the ins an outs of the legal aspects of law but make that effort, black masses will not rally behind the insinuator for justice.

26) They are the least number of land owners even in countries where they are

The majority, it has been shown that black people Owen less land than any other race.

It can be said that there are some communities where in outside races come in an buy property.

Black people having been resident there the longest an still naw Owen any land.

Many black people so it would seem if a lump of money was obtained they would look at the amount of years rent this money could pay as oppose to buying their Owen home.

In many cases such things are done out of arrogance toward one another.

27) Very seldom is a black child brought up by both parents being under the same roof.

Not often do black children get to be brought up by both parents.

Many times or so society calls it a broken home.

This is where black children grow.

Black children have time an time aging grown up with mother an father nowhere to be seen, physical an financial.

This is an occurrence that has taken place from as far back as you want go right up to date.

In some parts of the world it is viewed a strange occurrence for father to be involved in the upbringing of a black child.

28) SINGLE BLACK MOTHERS TEND TO MOLD THEIR CHILDREN TO BE JUST LIKE THEM.

Dress manner even response to society.

Many a times throughout society in many different countries single black women mold their children intensely.

Many times the children end up looking like sister an brothers of these type parents every aspect of life is discussed with her children many times advice given by the children is followed to the letter by most single black mothers.

29) BLACK MEN ARE MORE THAN LIKELY TO HAVE CHILDREN THROUGH MORE THAN ONE WOMAN

This can take place in many black men's life, no matter what their back round or the walk of life they may come From, Black men of several denomination's the good and the bad alike

30) Black children are more than likely to grow without ever meeting their father

A vast majority never really get to meet even know their father as a person.

For some real trivial purpose many times black children don't have I interrelation with their fathers.

This being an issue instituted by the mother much of the time.

In lots of cases the father takes no interests in his responsibility an stay away from the child or children.

In lots of cases the father is chased away by family friends an associates of the mother of these children

32) Black men tend to get their women high on whatever substance the use to get high.

Most people get high some way or the other an many times in relationships when both parties get high its usually on the man's choice of drug.

It can be said in regard to many relationships that exists that when they meet she didn't even smoke cigarettes an look at her now.

Such things can occur even when it is concerning alcohol an all manner of intoxicating drink.

33) BLACK PEOPLE HAVE THE OLDEST CITIES ON THE PLANET.

Not saying that these cities are inhabited or in use today but the fact that we as a race of people organized an put together a social program on all levels in regard to social livening.

The ruins of these cities are in existences they may be buried but many forms of social living were put in place by us black people in these cities.

There by solidifying the fact that black people have the oldest cities on earth.

Yet we are just occupants today in far away lands.

34) Friends close associates an family of black people will cause you troubles like woo

An still go on like you an them a friend fe life, dem having excess to your affairs sometimes even your possessions they will poke at disrupt the program then look pon you as if duh?

35) Its sad to say but lots of people in the black race is beyond help due to the fact

That your assistance will be viewed by them as though you've been tricked.

When in reality they need that assistance to go from A too B.

Many times it can be said lots of black people have very little or none ability to show appreciation for favors an gifts lots of individuals in the black race resort to a state of

Mind as though life owes them all of its nescietyies, in lots of cases this mind set is developed in the family home.

From such occurrences this mind set is carried throughout life.

36) THEY WON'T STOP TURNING NEIGHBORHOODS THEY MOVE INTO TOO GHETTOS

Many a times they move in neighborhoods an start making a nuances of them self's in many ways.

They do all sorts of activity which removes a element of security from said neighborhoods.

This element of security having been established by no one doing the things that are being done since their arrival in to the neighborhoods

37) THEY HAVE THE MOST TRUE STORIES TO TELL FROM LIFE EXPERIENCE AN WON'T WRITE NO BOOKS MAKE NO FILMS.

Black people the world over seem as though they are always faced with the hardest road toward some sort of relaxed an stable environment.

Financial an physical black people go through trials an turmoil in just putting a stable environment together to live in.

Whole families can be faced with such turmoil there by making for the more points of view fro the making of books and films.

The many stories that can be told.

38) THEY WILL HOLD YOU TO A MINOR DEBT BUT ARE THE BIGGEST DEBT CARRIERS.

It has been said in some circles that its more comforting to know that you

Owe a million dollars to a white man before owing a black man just ten pounds they will scorn you, bad mouth you, speak all manner of bad talk behind your back even though the money was put in your hand on a friendship basis.

No matter the amount of the loan.

39) THEY CONSTANTLY TRY TO INTIMIDATE ONE ANOTHER FOR ALL SORTS OF NAÏVE AN TRIVIAL REASONS

Male an female will try to intimidate an manipulate people, new faces an present associates.

In look talk even group association is a few of the ways in which they will try to intimidate other people such a practices is a constant in some communities, this is carried out toward family, friends and strangers given the opportunity.

40) THEY WON'T STOP BEING PASSIVE TO PEOPLE OF LIGHTER SKIN COLOR.

Time an time aging black people will do their out most to the next black face but will bend over backward for any one of fairer skin color white yellow in some cases brown.

A black skin person having been told to do something by a next black person will huff puff an insist they don't have to do but a person of lighter skin tells them the same thing they'll jump to it an in some cases think you the next black person has to do likewise.

41) THEY HAVE THE LARGEST NUMBER OF ADULTS IN ANY GIVEN COUNTRY THAT HAVE NO COMPUTER ABILITY.

They take no steps to change this even in cases of free access to computers in a lot of cases you'll find when steps are taken to change this a large portion of the community will taught an tease as if it's a bad thing to learn a new skill.

42) BEING THE MAJORITY IN ANY GIVEN PROFESSION I.E. BUS DRIVER HOTEL WORKER TRAIN WORKERS.

You will find very little unity amongst black people in such cases in light of the fact that such settings can work to the benefit of those and other black people the amounts of money made in such places if x amount was to be put together some sort of fund could be established to materialize their Owen bus company an the rest.

43) THEY WOULD TAKE UP SOMETHING ORIGINATED BY ANOTHER RACE AN GO ON LIKE THEY

Originated it, lots of religions having been taken up by black people an many ways of livening which have been adapted to by black people will be put to inquiring people as though this thing was originated by the black race.

44) Constantly black people allow them selves to be denied an decremented

Against, in London you see in many places black people being subject to things no other race is subject to this is also done in other parts of the world, housing, jobs, financial assistance even charitable hand outs you'll find black people are scrutinized an denied many things.

Such denial can be found even in asking for police assistances against injustices being exerted by other races against black people.

This can only end if we pull together as a people.

45) THEY FOLLOW OPPRESSIVE RULES AN REGULATIONS TO THE LETTER WHEN IT COMES TO APPLYING IT TO THEM ONE ANOTHER.

In many parts of the world black people operating public forms of transport subject other black people to intense scrutiny they even denied them access if they are short on fare an that will applied to all age brackets but all other races upon encounter of people of their race, free access is given to all age brackets.

Such oppressiveness can be found in all sorts of situations it an be viewed as though if you give one black person the chance to beat the next black person, such a opportunity is jumped to time an time aging.

46) Daily In London many black people watch public TV which is BBC.

Of which puts very few black people on or in their programs.

TV license is paid for constantly by lots of black people an many other gadgets to

Enhances that TV, viewing of public broadcasting.

Yet through the course of the day you can literally count the amount of black people on your fingers that appear on their channel.

Yet black people sit in front of those TVs constantly.

47) A VAST MAJORITY OF SINGLE BLACK MAN HAVING LIVED A PRODUCTIVE

Life tend to turn to drug taking when the hectic aspect of their life starts to decrees with in many cities of the world men in the age bracket of late forties up to their sixties you can find a large number spend lots of time chasseing drugs mainly hard drugs all to often a whole life style will be adopted in the drug criteria by such men.

You can find this is done by black women in some cases.

48) MANY BLACK MEN INVOLVED IN THE ILLEGAL DRUG TRADE TEND NOT TO APPLY THEIR FINANCIAL GAINS TO PRODUCTIVE MEANS

Time an time aging you can easily find a black man who has spent many years involved in drug trafficking an has little or nothing to show for his efforts upon reaching a certain age, lots of times money comes an goes, on the job criteria an work association is where lots of his money is spent.

49) Black people won't stop joining oppressive organization of which in flicks

Oppression on their fellow man.

Police is a prime example where in a function having been put on in a black community police will attend after a certain hour many times in a aggressive manner.

Same function on in a different races hood an you get a all different response to the offenders from the police.

Lots of times no sort of oppressiveness is shown or exerted toward other races, [so it seems only black people.]

50) Black people world wide for decades will not join their finance to build up Africa

Many parts of Africa are awaiting development yet black people outside of Africa will not take steps to do such things.

Very few black people outside of certain circles have knowledge of such things the few that know of such things will not take steps to make it known on a larger scale.

If for any thing to see what type of response will be give by a vast majority having knowledge of such facts.

Many parts of Africa have areas allotted for black people outside of Africa to develop yet no steps are taken to make such things a realty.

In some parts of Africa even finances have been put in place for such things yet no steps are taken to make something out of such opportunities.

51) BLACK PEOPLE WILL NOT ACKNOWLEDGE THE FACT THAT WE AS A RACE HAVE MORE RHYTHM THAN ALL OTHER RACES.

In acknowledging of this should make some avenues more accessible for a bigger portion of blacks to get involved in many fields of entertainment.

Where in to put our product out to market.

For the many millions of dollars pounds sterling all currencies in black people's pockets there should be some sort of gate way for the literally brook black person to get their form of entertainment out to the public.

To say it so it covers more than entertainment lets say craft.

52) BLACK PEOPLE DO NOT OFTEN USE THE POWER OF THE COURTS IN PURSUIT OF JUSTICE.

Many organizations do an will push an miss treat black people to the extent of outright injustice.

Still a black person will say don't worry about it, when they have all right to purse justice through the court system

54) MANY BLACK FAMILIES FALL APART DUE TO THE FACT THAT

when the youth become young adults they tend to rebel against authority.

The first form of authority they rebel against is mom an dad.

Having walked away from that, had their way it could be said they feel they are ready to take on the world so before long a vast majority end up in the court system, then jail.

55) BLACK MEN TEND TO TAKE A DELIGHT IN HAVING AFFAIRS WITH FEMALES FAR UNDER THEIR

Age bracket.

Lots of young black ladies fall victim to such men.

Such things has happen for generations.

In some parts of Africa this is called a Traditions, in some parts of the developed world this is viewed as posh, cool, a must have accessory.

56) Black people tend to let family disagreements stay a issue far beyond a sensible length of time.

For each and every individual on earth at some time or the other had to

Rely on other than family.

Still given first chance to jump at family their off.

An will dissociate with them for good.

Lots of times for the most trivial reasons.

57) BLACK PEOPLE TEND NOT TO NURTURE THE FAMILY UNIT.

They will spend time with family regularly but the first chance to disrespect one another their off this moment of disrespect of can turn in to the biggest of disputes an eventually into non-association with one another.

Where in if the family unit was a real concern then certain issues will not go out of control to the extant of non-association with each other.

58) BLACK PEOPLE TEND TO ACT AS THOUGH THEY KNOW A PERSON THROUGH HAVING BEEN TOLD SOME FORM OF GOSSIP ABOUT THAT PERSON BY ANOTHER.

They will speak as if they where in association with that person.

Many times such manner is used to prevent new friendships from starting.

Black women do such things often when relationships fall apart.

She proclaims to the world her side of the story even thought all that she will talk to have no association with the one whom she speaks about.

Now all she has spoke to start to go on in a manner as if they to have been in conflict with the individual whom they have been spoken to about.

59) Black men tend to be argumentative with their ladies in attempts

To escape their financial obligations to her an any youth they may have.

A black lady trying to get money out of a black man toward the maintenance of her child or children is often met with a argumentative response.

In many cases mom has to be dad too.

It can be said; upon notifying dad that hell soon be that[a dad]he be gone.

60) MANY BLACK MEN HAVE ONE CHILD AN DUE TO THEIRS AN THE MOTHERS INABILITY TO WORK OUT SOME SORT OF MONEY PROGRAMME FOR THE YOUTH THEY STAY AWAY FROM THE YOUTH

Many cases the mother will not use her earnings to care for this child but demand that the father pay all expense in regard to this child or children having no way of changing mothers view the father decides to stay out of the child's life.

61) BLACK PEOPLE TEND TO DESPISE THAT WHICH IDENTIFIES WITH THEIR HISTORY

A vast amount of black people in the developed world anywhere outside of Africa have a mental picture of African descent as a thing where in their ancestors lived like animals or worst.

There by you can not associate them with such things on any level.

Any form of association that exists was a long time ago a so dem would tell you many black people will proclaim due to their birth, dem not African, their birth.

Having taken place out side of Africa then they have no affiliation with Africa.

62) A VAST MAJORITY OF BLACK PEOPLE DON'T LIKE TO HEAR ABOUT CONCEPTS OF INDEPENDENCE.

Put a idea to a black person about financial independence an they change.

Some will get argumentative an some will try an brand you crazy to think you can make a living out side of a pay check many black people are happy like woo to get a regular pay check it is said in some black communities if you don't have a job u need to get one.

63) MANY TIMES BLACK WOMEN ENFORCE DEPENDENCE ON THEIR CHILDREN SO AS TO MAKE THE CHILD DEPENDENT ON THEM LONGER THAN NEED BE

The many gifts the lumps of money the fact that the child can lay lay bout the house like every thing in the house is free is encouraged by the mother

All these things been done so as to keep the child in her reach or say her home.

Many times she will go to their aid if they have their own home in spite of the fact that they are more than able to care for themselves.

This act of going to their aid can be physical as well financial.

Lots of times their last penny will be contributed to her child or children for their wants or needs

64) BLACK PEOPLE TEND TO SPEND FAR TO MUCH MONEY ON A LIFE STYLE THEY DON'T NEED.

A large number of black people will spend every earned penny on a profile that is purely theatrical.

Some parts of their life style can be eliminated an not missed on a necessity basis.

As has been said; them love keep up with the Jones's.

What a laugh.

Cause a we set the trend.

65) LOTS OF BLACK PEOPLES CHILDREN WILL NOT DO HALF THE THINGS THEIR PARENTS HAVE DONE FOR THEM
FOR THIERS PARENTS

Meaning a large number of black youth will view it a NO NO to do for their parents.

To spend money on their parents is out of the question lots of black peoples children see it as a outrageous though to think they would spend money on their parents an will demand they are left alone so such things can't be addressed

66) Black people have the most natural talent

An don't get involved in entertainment, it can be said an has been done you can take a black youth male or female out of the general public an with a little direction an instruction it's a good thing you can develop the next Michael J.

We were entertainers whilst we were in chains many times a mother murdered in front on her youth was considered a form of entertainment many times we were the life of the party in many occasions by our will an others desirer to laugh

67) Black people the world over are faced with the same obstacles but never acknowledge it.

If some sort of unity was established between black people then lots of times when one of us is faced with injustice it can be identified for what it is.

We will an have many times acknowledged to we one another that at some time or the other we have been faced with the same type of injustice on a singular term of which will be put by us as a thing to not be disputed as if we are required to stay under oppression an road blocks

68) BLACK MEN AN MALE YOUTH THE WORLD OVER ARE ALMOST ALWAYS LOOKED AT BY SOCIETY AS A PROBLEM.

in lots of cities through out the world we are the only ones stopped searched or even followed up an down in our vehicles.

Our spots of social gathering are constantly invaded by police with the insinuation that we are the only ones in society with something illegal in our possessions

69) Many of the great men of the bible were black men.

But society teaches different.

You can get scholars an so called researchers of the bible saying that this an that man was not black as if it'll be a crime to make mention of the facts you can find black scholars saying the same sort of nonsense, along with many Black People, world wide.

70) THINGS THAT THE BLACK RACE HAS DONE AN CAN DO HAS NEVER BEEN COMPARED TO OR DONE BY OTHER RACES.

Just our bounce back from slavery to the many fine people that we are should show the world that we are a peculiar people.

It can be said black man has held every job known to society as we know it to date.

Yet we are happy with one month of acknowledging our greatness.

71) **S**OME ORGANIZATIONS HAVE HAD BLACK PEOPLE
WORKING FOR THEM FOR YEARS YET THERE HAS NEVER
BEEN A BLACK PERSON IN CHARGE ON ANY LEVEL.

If black people was united such issues could be addressed an questioned even put in to court for this can be viewed as a human rights issue for its long over due

72) Some organizations if having a black person in authority would make a large number of staff want to quit.

A large number of people in society having no regard or passion for the black race will not work a nine to five if a black person was in charge.

So if there was some sort of unity amongst black people this form of prejudice could be addressed many forms of prejudice will not be so easily hidden.

If you take time an listen to them an those who don't have black skin talk amongst them one another, oh you will, Black person you're not that like amongst then. Trust you me.

73) Black people won't stop trying to insinuate that I'm' better off than you.

Black people have played that game amongst them one another for hundreds of years.

Even in light of the fact that most are in the same boat financial.

You have some with no personal wealth just true them in the company of extremely wealthy person an spend these peoples money so they insinuate their stupidness.

Their arrogance in lots of cases it can be said their lack of intelligence. Sight.

74) Most religion all over the world bear a similar format in their concept of pleasing god or lets say their deity.

With in most concepts god is some deity who is not really associated by man.

Except for the Christian way of which depicts god as a man black man is the only one who has the legitimate right to say god is one of us.

But he won't an most of them are insulted when being encouraged to think so.

Trying to get lots of Black people to acknowledge just the fact that God is a man is like trying to pull teeth that are not ready to come out.

75) HAVING SAID THAT MOST RELIGIONS FOLLOW A SIMILAR FORMAT

let me point out that the black race is the only race that god himself has chosen to show himself as a man amongst men.

This can be examined an proven from many different points in the Rasta way of life an his acknowledging of the divinity of His Imperial Majesty Emperor Haile Selassie I.

Jah Rastafari

Many a question can be answered on such a avenue but are seldom.

Let it be said even if we as people did not acknowledge His Majesty's divinity an just made a constant enforcement of the things he spoke of as a person, could and will make even help the individual to be that much more the better person cause many speeches were put out by his Imperial Majesty in regard to many different aspects of life even human interaction an self upliftment this being some of the things we really can use some direction in as humans. What ? onna can't see that ?

Taken up by a great number of the black race which occurrences should bring us to the fact that

JAH LIVE.